MEXICO

Marshall Cavendish
Benchmark

New York

Written by: Leslie Jermyn and Fiona Conboy
Editors: Peter Mavrikis, Cheryl Sim
Publisher: Michelle Bisson
Series Designer: Benson Tan

Photo research by Thomas Khoo

Originated and designed by Marshall Cavendish International (Asia) Pte Ltd
Copyright © 2011 Marshall Cavendish International (Asia) Pte Ltd
Published by Marshall Cavendish Benchmark
An imprint of Marshall Cavendish Corporation
All rights reserved.

This publication represents the opinions and views of the authors based on
Leslie Jermyn and Fiona Conboy's personal experience, knowledge, and research.
The information in this book serves as a general guide only. The authors and
publisher have used their best efforts in preparing this book and disclaim liability
rising directly and indirectly from the use and application of this book.

Other Marshall Cavendish Offices:
Marshall Cavendish International (Asia) Pte Ltd, 1 New Industrial Road,
Singapore 536196 • Marshall Cavendish International (Thailand) Co Ltd.
253 Asoke, 12th Flr, Sukhumvit 21 Road, Klongtoey Nua, Wattana,
Bangkok 10110, Thailand • Marshall Cavendish (Malaysia) Sdn Bhd,
Times Subang, Lot 46, Subang Hi-Tech Industrial Park, Batu Tiga,
40000 Shah Alam, Selangor Darul Ehsan, Malaysia

Marshall Cavendish is a trademark of Times Publishing Limited.
All websites were available and accurate when this book was sent to press.

Library of Congress Cataloging-in-Publication Data
Jermyn, Leslie.
Mexico / Leslie Jermyn and Fiona Conboy.
p. cm. — (Welcome to my country)
Summary: "An overview of the history, geography, government, economy,
language, people, and culture of Mexico. Includes numerous color photos,
a detailed map, useful facts, and detailed resource section"
—Provided by publisher.
Includes index.
ISBN 978-1-60870-157-5
[1. Mexico—Juvenile literature.] I. Conboy, Fiona. II. Title.
F1208.5.J46 2011
972—dc22   2010001204

Printed in Malaysia
135642

PHOTO CREDITS
Alamy: 12, 22, 25, 34, 42
Art Directors & TRIP Photo Library: 24
Bes Stock: 30
David Simson: 3 (top), 3 (centre), 5, 14, 21, 27 (bottom),
    28 (both), 37
Focus Team: 27 (top)
Getty Images: 23 (top), 35, 38
Hutchison Library: 1, 2, 7, 19, 29, 32, 40
Liba Taylor: 4
Photolibrary: cover, 8, 10, 11, 15, 16, 18,20, 23 (bottom), 36, 39
Tan Chung Lee: 13, 31, 41
The Image Bank: 17
Topham Picturepoint: 3 (bottom), 6, 9, 26, 33

Contents

Words that appear in the glossary are printed in **boldface** type the first time they occur in the text.

In Mexican villages, donkeys are a slow but common form of transportation.

Welcome to Mexico!

Many years ago, Mexico was ruled by the Aztecs and the Maya. Today, Mexico's population is a mixture of Spanish and Indian **ancestry**. Let's learn about the colorful history of Mexico and its people.

Mexican performers reenacting Aztec dances at festival time.

The Flag of Mexico

The Mexican flag has green, white, and red bands. The central **crest** is an Aztec symbol of an eagle eating a snake. Huitzilopochtli, the god of war, told the Aztecs to build their capital where they found an eagle eating a snake. Today, the capital is called Mexico City.

The Land

Mexico lies at the very southern border of the United States. It is a long country shaped like a hook. The feature of the land changes from north to south and east to west. It has dry deserts and tropical rain forests, volcanoes and snowcapped mountains, and swampy **lagoons** and white sandy beaches.

This volcanic mountain is in southern Mexico. It is called Mount Popocatépetl, or "smoking mountain."

The cactus is a common plant in the Mexican desert where it can survive the dry heat.

The Mexican Plateau is an enormous plain stretching from the north of the country to the south. This is the most populated part of Mexico. Arid deserts occupy the north. Farther south where there is heavy rainfall, lush green forests come into sight. On either side of the plateau are two mountain ranges running along each coastline—the Sierra Madre Occidental to the west and the Sierra Madre Oriental to the east.

Climate

The weather in Mexico changes from one part of the country to another. The climate is hot and dry in the south and in the northern deserts. It is much colder high in the mountains.

The rainy season runs from May to August, when it rains almost every day in the central valleys. Tropical **hurricanes** occur on both coasts every year.

These monarch butterflies **migrate** to Mexico from the United States and Canada to escape the winter.

Coatimundi are members of the raccoon family. They climb trees in search of food.

Plants and Animals

You can see many different **species** of animals in Mexico. Coatimundi live in the lowland trees, jaguars stalk the rain forests, and whales swim in the warm oceans.

Many plants can also be found in Mexico. The cactus is common because it can survive desert conditions. Some people even eat cactus plants in spite of their prickly skin!

History

Hundreds of years ago, Mexico was ruled by native Indian tribes. The early Maya civilization occupied the Yucatán Peninsula of Mexico and flourished between 300–900 CE before mysteriously losing power. They were followed by the Aztecs, who by the early 1500s had become one of the most powerful tribes. As a result, many other Indians became unhappy with their **domination**. In 1519, explorer Hernán Cortés arrived from Spain and defeated the Aztecs with the help of Indians he recruited. He named Mexico *New Spain*.

In 1519, Hernán Cortés attacked the Aztec capital of **Tenochtitlan** (tay-NOSH-teet-lan) and took Montezuma, the Aztec king, as his hostage. Two years later, the Aztec Empire collapsed.

Miguel Hidalgo, who is more famously known as Father Hidalgo, started the Mexican war for independence in 1810. He was killed in battle in 1811.

Freedom for Mexico

Early in the nineteenth century, the Mexican people wanted independence from Spain. After a ten-year war, an agreement was signed, and Mexico was freed from Spain's control.

In 1858, **civil war** raged between the Catholic Church and the people from one side of the government known as the liberals. An Indian named Benito Juárez led the people through the war. Juárez and his followers won this civil war.

This wall painting of Zapata shows how powerful the people thought this leader was during the Mexican Revolution.

The Mexican Revolution

After Juárez's death, Porfirio Díaz became president and ruled Mexico for thirty-five years. During this time, the poor grew poorer, and in 1910 there was a **rebellion** by the **peasants**, led by Emiliano Zapata and Francisco "Pancho" Villa. The rebellion turned into a violent war—known as the Mexican Revolution—that lasted ten years and killed 1.5 million people.

Mexico Today

After the revolution, many Mexican families moved from the countryside to the cities. Others stayed behind to farm the land and sell the crops in local towns and villages.

Felipe de Jesús Calderón Hinojosa is Mexico's current leader until the next **election** in 2012. He is improving housing, education, and health care for all Mexicans.

After a farmer feeds his family, the rest of the produce is sold at the market.

A True Indian Hero

Benito Juárez was **orphaned** at three years of age. He worked in the fields until he was twelve, when he decided to get an education. He graduated from law school and started a career in politics. Juárez became president of Mexico in 1861 and stayed in power for fourteen years. He was the first powerful Indian in independent Mexico and died a national hero.

Mexico was invaded by the French in 1863. Four years later, Juárez and his government defeated the French in a series of battles and regained control of the country.

"Pancho" Villa (**center**) was considered a bandit by many during his lifetime but is now a legendary figure.

The Legend of "Pancho"

Francisco "Pancho" Villa's parents also died when he was very young. He didn't go to school, but he taught himself to read and write. He was a courageous and famous soldier in the revolution. Pancho continued fighting for the rights of the peasants of Mexico after the war. In 1923, he was **ambushed** and killed by outlaws on his ranch.

The Government and the Economy

Presidential Power

Mexico is ruled by a president who is voted into office every six years. Each president of Mexico can hold power for only one term. The president's office is in the National Palace in Mexico City, the capital of the country.

The National Palace in Mexico City is located in one of the world's largest plazas. The plaza—or public square—is called the *zócalo* (SO-kah-loh).

Every young Mexican male must complete military service that lasts for a year.

Mexican Politics

There are three governmental branches in Mexico—the executive, legislative, and judicial. The government is run by one dominant political party. The president is the head of that party. He appoints qualified citizens to serve as **diplomats**, chief military officers, and judges. The main political party in Mexico today is the Institutional Revolutionary Party, which has won every election until 2000, when it was defeated by the Alliance for Change in the presidential election. The Alliance for Change included the National Party and the Green Ecological Party of Mexico, which are two other popular political parties in the Mexican government.

Many Mexican children in poor, rural areas work on the family's land.

Farming the Land

Agriculture is a big industry in Mexico. Some families have small plots of land where they grow their own food, but there are many large areas of farmland in Mexico still owned by a few rich people. Large farms grow fruit, rice, and cotton, but sugarcane and coffee are the most important crops. Most of the sugarcane stays in Mexico, but much of the coffee is sold to other countries.

Drilling for Oil

Mexico has many natural **resources**, such as oil and gas. Most of the oil is produced in the northeastern part of the country. A system of pipelines transports the oil to the rest of Mexico and to the border of the United States. Gold, silver, and copper are also mined in Mexico and exported around the world. Mexico trades with the United States, Canada, Japan, Spain, France, Germany, and Brazil.

Oil was discovered in Mexico in 1974. Mexico is the largest producer of oil in Latin America, and in 2008, it was the world's seventh-largest oil producer.

People and Lifestyle

Mestizos

After Mexico's independence from Spain, the Spanish and the Indians lived peacefully with one another and began to have children together. Children with one Spanish parent and one Indian parent are called *mestizos* (mess-TEE-zos). Today, mestizos make up the majority of the Mexican population.

Children at a Mexican school. Today, most Mexicans are metizos.

Mexican families are very close. They work hard together.

Indians

There are still many small Indian communities in Mexico. These Indians live in villages where they have their own culture, languages, and customs.

Mexican families like this one enjoy bonding over a meal.

One Big Happy Family

Family life is important in Mexico. Children, parents, and grandparents often live together. Both parents in Mexican families go out to work, especially those living in the city areas. During the week, everyone in the family eats lunch together. The special day of the week is Sunday, when friends and family visit, share a meal, or even have a picnic!

From the Cradle to the Altar

When a baby is born to a Catholic family in Mexico, the child is baptized by a priest. Years later, at the age of about twelve, children are **confirmed** in the Church.

Most Mexican couples who wish to marry have a traditional church wedding. Weddings in Mexico tend to be large and are often followed with a reception that includes lots of music, dancing, and traditional foods.

Children traditionally wear white for a confirmation ceremony.

Mexican weddings are festive occasions.

Education

School is free in Mexico, and children must attend until at least the sixth grade. At fourteen, they decide whether or not to continue their education at secondary school.

After secondary school, students can continue their education by going to a university. Most of the universities in Mexico are located in the big towns and cities. The first Mexican university was opened in Mexico City in 1551 by the King of Spain.

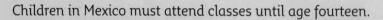

Children in Mexico must attend classes until age fourteen.

Some children earn extra money for their families as street musicians.

Some Mexican families are poor and cannot afford to buy the books and clothes their children need for school. Others keep their children home to work the land. The Mexican government encourages all children to go to school.

Gods and Goddesses

Before the Spanish arrived in Mexico, Indians worshiped many different gods. One of the gods was Quetzalcoatl (KAYT-sal-koh-AT-ul), the Aztec god of wind and breath. When Hernán Cortés arrived in Mexico, the Aztecs thought he was Quetzalcoatl because he looked so strange to them. Cortés may have conquered the Aztecs because the Indians were so afraid of him.

Quetzalcoatl means "feather-covered snake" in the Indian language of Nahuatl.

Some Catholic churches in Mexico, like this one built in 1690, are filled with elaborate carvings painted in gold.

The Catholic Church

After Cortés's conquest of the Aztecs, Catholic missionaries arrived from Spain to teach the native Indians about Christianity. Catholic churches were built throughout Mexico. Today, over 90 percent of the Mexican population is Roman Catholic.

The Virgin Mary is very important to Mexican Catholics. They call her the Virgin of Guadalupe. In 1754, Pope Benedict XIV declared December 12 a special feast day in her honor.

This image of the Virgin Mary is displayed on an enormous banner outside the Basilica of Guadalupe in Mexico City on her feast day.

Language

Spanish

The national language of Mexico is Spanish. It is taught in schools. Television shows and radio broadcasts nationwide are in Spanish.

Mexican Spanish has three different dialects. Each **dialect** comes from a region—Chilango Spanish from south-central Mexico, Norteño Spanish from northern Mexico, and Yucateco Spanish from Yucatán, the home of the Mayan civilization. The Spanish language spoken in Yucatán contains some Mayan words.

This billboard is written in Spanish and English to aid foreign tourists.

Most Mexican newspapers are printed in Spanish.

Even if two people speak different Spanish dialects, they will be able to understand one another.

Indian Languages

Spanish is not the only language spoken in Mexico. The word Mexico comes from the Aztec language, Nahuatl. Many Spanish words spoken today, such as *tortilla* (tor-TEE-yaa), and *tamale* (tah-MAH-lay) are **derived** from Nahuatl. There are about fifty Indian languages still spoken in Mexico by a small number of native Indians.

Arts

Before the Spanish arrived in Mexico, native Indian civilizations produced many styles of art. They created sculptures of gods, bright wall paintings called murals, and masks made of gold and silver decorated with colorful stones.

The Indians built huge pyramid-shaped temples in stone, but most of them were destroyed by the Spanish.

This ancient temple is found in a city called Teotihuacan and was built by its early inhabitants, the Teotihuacanos. When the Aztecs arrived centuries later, they named it the Pyramid of the Sun due to its triangular shape.

Huge *Churrigueresque* carvings of saints and elaborate columns decorate the front of this cathedral in Zacatecas.

A New Style

After the arrival of the Spanish, a new style of architecture appeared in Mexico. **Churrigueresque** (choo-REE-ger-ESK) featured elaborate carvings in stone.

In the twentieth century, Spanish and Indian art styles were combined depicting the European and Indian heritage of the Mexican people.

Music

No celebration takes place in Mexico without music. The most popular style is *norteña* (nor-TAYN-ya), a mixture of sounds from Europe and Mexico. *Tejano* (teh-HAHN-oh) is a combination of Mexican and American music. **Mariachi** (mah-ree-AH-chee) bands take their name from the word marriage because they used to perform at weddings. Today, they are popular at many occasions.

There are eight musicians in a *mariachi* band playing guitars, violins, and trumpets.

One of the most famous Mexican dance troupes is the Ballet Folklorico from Mexico City. They perform all around the world.

Dance

Mexicans also love to dance. Each region in the country has its own dances that are energetically performed in brightly colored costumes. The dances usually originate from either Spanish or Indian heritage.

Leisure Time

Fiestas are very important to the Mexican people. They are usually religious celebrations held near a church. People wear traditional dress and enjoy dancing and feasting. There are so many fiestas in Mexico that probably somewhere in the country, a fiesta is celebrated every day!

Mexican children love to put on their special festival costumes for a fiesta.

Piñatas look like oversized toys and are found in different shapes like clowns, monsters, or animals.

Party Time

One of the longest celebrations in Mexico is called *posada* (po-SAH-da). This occurs during Christmastime, when processions through the streets represent Mary and Joseph's journey to Bethlehem. Children enjoy a treat called **piñata** (peen-YAH-tah)—a hollow figure filled with sweets, which they hit with a stick until it bursts open.

Sports

Fútbol (FOOT-bohl) is Mexico's national sport. It is played throughout the country in towns and villages. Children play *fútbol*, also known as soccer, from an early age, and schools hold tournaments with one another. Baseball is popular in Mexico, too. Mexican teams compete in an annual event called the Caribbean World Series, which they have won several times.

Mexican children love to play *fútbol*, or soccer.

The *matador* waves a cape in front of the bull to make it charge at him.

Bullfighting

The sport of bullfighting came to Mexico from Spain. The bullfighter, called a *matador*, has to kill the bull with a sword. First, the bull is weakened with **lances** and sticks carried by men which are called *picadors* (pee-KAH-dors). Although many people consider it a cruel, inhumane sport, bullfighting is the most popular spectator event in Mexico.

The Day of the Dead

This festival is probably the most important Indian religious holiday in Mexico. It is a day to remember loved ones who have passed away. Food is left out for the dead by their families. People believe that the dead eat the "spirit" or nutrients, of the food. The next day, everyone celebrates with a feast. The celebration of the spirits of the dead began in ninth-century Europe and came to Mexico from Spain.

A tradition on Easter Saturday is to hang life-sized dummies of Judas in the streets and set them on fire. Judas betrayed Christ at the Last Supper so he is thought of as evil.

On the Day of the Dead, some people carry large skeleton puppets!

Holy Week

Easter celebrations last for one week in Mexico. This is Holy Week, and it honors the death of Christ on the cross. In many villages, the crucifixion is acted out on Good Friday. On Easter Saturday, an **effigy**, or model, of Judas is burned. Sometimes the model is gigantic in size and wears a mask. On Easter Sunday, Mexicans have special family feasts.

Food

Mexican food is a wonderful mixture of produce from throughout the world. Garlic came from Spain, crusty bread from France, sausages from Germany, and pasta from Italy.

Mexico has introduced much of its own foods to the rest of the world, too. Corn, tomatoes, potatoes, chocolate, vanilla, chilies, and peanuts originated in Mexico.

Tortillas are a staple part of the diet in Mexico and are eaten at most meals.

In city markets, fruit drinks are served from large jars.

Mexican Drinks

Corn is even used to make special fruit drinks in Mexico. Tortilla flour—made from corn—is mixed with water and various fruit juices and served over ice as a refreshing thirst quencher.

Mexicans drink a lot of coffee. It is very strong, so they like to drink it with plenty of sugar. Hot chocolate originated in Mexico, and it is a popular breakfast or dinner drink.

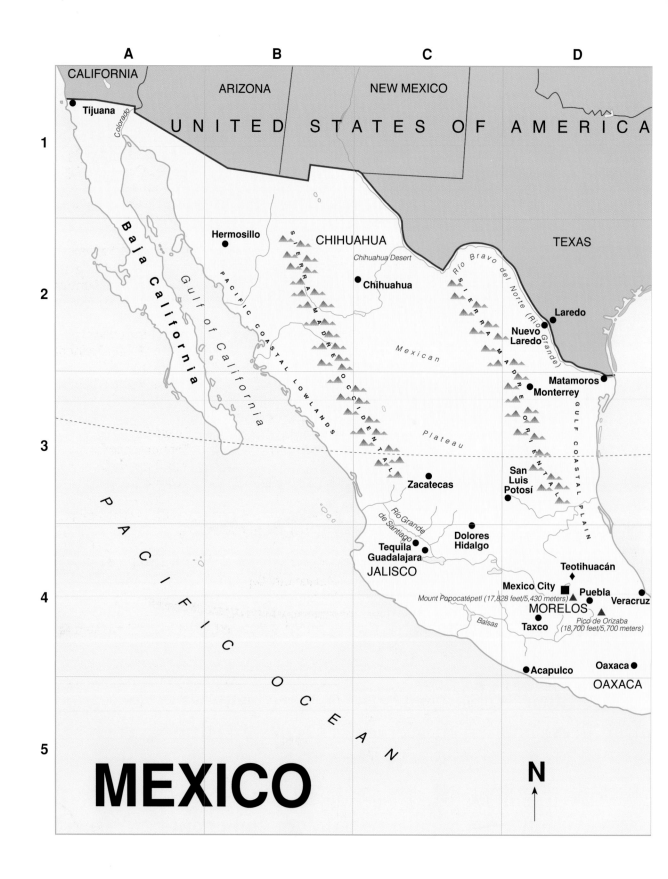

MEXICO

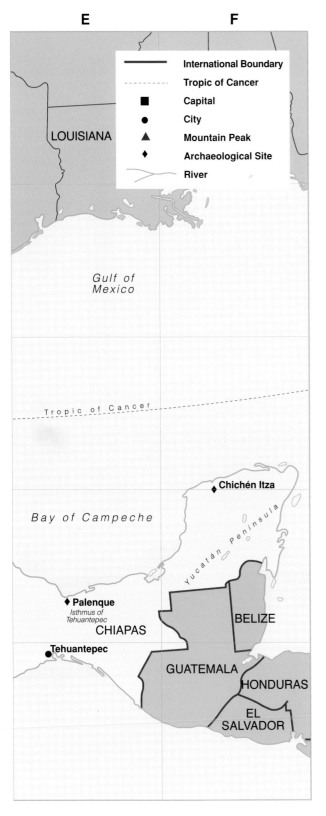

Acapulco D4

Baja California A2–3
Balsas C4
Belize F4

Chiapas (state) E4
Chichén Itza F3–4
Chihuahua (state) B2–C2
Chihuahua Desert C2

Dolores Hidalgo C4

El Salvador F5

Guadalajara C4
Guatemala F5
Gulf of California A2-B3
Gulf Coastal Plain D3
Gulf of Mexico E2

Honduras F5

Jalisco (state) C4

Laredo D2

Mexican Plateau C2–C3
Mexico City D4
Monterrey D3
Morelos (state) D4
Mount Popocatépetl, D4

Nuevo Laredo D2

Oaxaca (state) D5

Pacific Coastal Lowlands B2–B3
Pacific Ocean A3–C5
Palenque E4
Pico de Orizaba D4
Puebla D4

Río Bravo del Norte (Rio Grande) C2–D2
Río Grande de Santiago C3–C4

San Luis Putosí D3
Sierra Madre Occidental B2–C3
Sierra Madre Oriental C2–D3

Taxco D4
Tehuantepec E5
Teotihuacán D4
Tequila C4
Tijuana A1
Tropic of Cancer E3

United States of America A1–F1

Veracruz D4

Yucatán Peninsula F4

Zacatecas C3

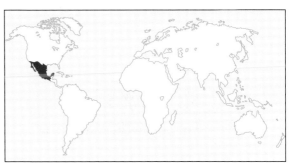

Quick Facts

Official Name United Mexican States

Capital Mexico City

Official Language Spanish

Population 111,211,789

Land Area 750,561 square miles/1,943,945 square kilometers

States Aguascalientes, Baja California (Norte and Sur), Campeche, Chiapas, Chihuahua, Coahuila, Colima, Durango, Guanajuato, Guerrero, Hidalgo, Jalisco, Michoacán, Morelos, Nayarit, Nuevo León, Oaxaca, Puebla, Querétaro, Quintana Roo, San Luis Potosí, Sinaloa, Sonora, Tabasco, Tamaulipas, Tlaxcala, Veracruz, Yucatán, Zacatecas

Highest Point Pico de Orizaba (18,700 feet/5,700 meters)

Major River Río Bravo del Norte (Rio Grande)

Main Religion Roman Catholic

Famous Leaders Benito Juárez, Migel Hidalgo y Costilla

Currency Mexico Peso (13.06 MXN = U.S. $1 in 2010)

The high cliffs of Acapulco are popular with daring divers.

Glossary

ambushed: Attacked by surprise.

ancestry: Family history.

Churrigueresque: An elaborate architectural style from the eighteenth century.

civil war: A war between two groups of citizens in the same country.

confirmed: Made part of a church, such as the Roman Catholic Church.

crest: An emblem or design on a flag or coat of arms.

derived: Created from another source.

dialect: Form of a language used in a particular area of a country.

diplomat: A government representative who deals with political problems in other countries.

domination: Having authority or power over someone else.

effigy: A model of a real person.

election: The formal vote to elect a government member or party.

hurricane: A violent, destructive tropical wind storm.

lagoon: Shallow pond.

lance: Long, sharp-tipped weapon.

mariachi: A type of Mexican music. The band is made up of violins, guitars, and trumpets.

mestizo: Person of mixed Spanish and Indian ancestry.

migrate: To travel from one area to another, usually to escape bad weather or to find food.

orphaned: Left alone as a child after the death of parents.

peasant: A very poor farm worker.

picador: Horse rider who stuns the bull with a lance in a bullfight.

piñata: A figure, usually made of papier-mache, that children break open with a stick to receive the candy inside.

rebellion: A fight against a government or ruler.

resource: Natural supply of materials, such as oil, gas, and coal.

species: A grouping of animals or plants that share similar characteristics.

Tenochtitlan: The capital city of the Aztecs, where Mexico City now lies.

For More Information

Books

Burt, Janet. *The Pacific North States of Mexico.* Broomall, PA: Mason Crest Publishers, 2008.

Hunter, Amy N. *The History of Mexico.* Broomall, PA: Mason Crest Publishers, 2008.

Kalman, Bobbie. *Mexico the Land.* New York: Crabtree Publishing Company, 2008.

Landau, Elaine. *True Book: Mexico.* New York: Scholastic Library Publishing, 2008.

Stein, R. Conrad. *Mexico.* New York: Scholastic Library Publishing, 2006.

Zronik, John Paul. *Hernando Cortés: Spanish Invader of Mexico.* New York: Crabtree Publishing Company, 2006.

DVDs

Discovery Atlas: Mexico Revealed. (Discovery Channel, 2008).

Global Wonders: Mexico. (Global Wonders, 2008).

Globe Trekker: Ultimate Mexico. (Pilot Productions, 2007).

Mexico's Great Pyramids. (A&E Home Video, 2009).

Mexico to the Max. (Questar, 2007).

Websites

www.atozkidsstuff.com/mexico.html

Part of this site is dedicated to such Mexican craft activities as making a donkey pinata, a paperbag poncho, a decorative beaded dish, and more.

www.facts-about-mexico.com

Easy-to-find sidebar topics include culture, people, religion, history, and food.

www.globaleye.org.uk/primary/eyeon/index.html

A colorful and appealing site that offers a snapshot of Mexico, complete with a unique profile of a Mexican family who live in the small village of Tocuaro.

www.theancientweb.com/explore/content.aspx?content_id=19

Learn about the ancient Mexican civilizations that first inhabited the country.

Index

The Making of a Champion

A World-Class
Judo Champion

Heinemann Library

Chicago, Illinois

Paul Mason

© 2004 Heinemann Library
a division of Reed Elsevier Inc.
Chicago, Illinois

Customer Service 888-454-2279

Visit our website at www.heinemannlibrary.com

Designed by Heinemann Library
Printed in China by WKT Company Limited.

08 07 06 05 04
10 9 8 7 6 5 4 3 2 1

Library of Congress Cataloging-in-Publication Data

Mason, Paul, 1967-
  A world-class judo champion / Paul Mason.
     p. cm. -- (Making of a champion)
Includes bibliographical references and index.
  ISBN 1-4034-4673-3 (Library Binding-hardcover) -- ISBN 1-4034-5534-1
(Paperback)
  1. Judo--Juvenile literature. [1. Judo.] I. Title. II. Series.
  GV1114.M373 2004
  796.815'2--dc22
                                     2003025997

Acknowledgments
The publishers would like to thank the following for permission to reproduce photographs:

p. 12 Action Plus, p 15 bottom; p. 33 David Hoffman Photo Library/Alamy; p. 4 Bob Willingham, p. 6 top, p. 7, p. 8, p. 9 top, p. 10, p. 11, p. 13 top, p. 13 bottom, p. 16, p. 17 bottom, p. 18 left, p. 18 right, p. 19, p. 20 (x 6), p. 21, p. 22, p. 23, p. 28, p. 29, p. 30, p. 31 top, p. 31 bottom, p. 34, p. 35, p. 38, p. 41; p. 5 top Jacques Langevin/Sygma/Corbis, p. 5 bottom, p. 27 top; p. 6 bottom DPA/Empics, p. 15 top Tony Marshall/Empics, p. 17 top Matthew Ashton/Empics, p. 36, p. 42 Sygma/Hekimian Julien/Empics, p. 43 top Prevosto Olivier/Empics; p. 14 L'Equipe, p. 37; p. 25 top Rex Features/Sipa Press; p. 27 bottom Stanley Chou/Allsport/Getty News and Sport; p. 9 bottom Trevor Clifford/Harcourt Education; p. 24 Kimimasa Mayama/Reuters, p. 25 bottom Jack Dabaghian/Reuters, p. 39 Kimimasa Mayama/Reuters, p. 43 bottom Philippe Wojazer/Reuters; p. 32 John Heseltine/SPL; p. 40 unknown.

Cover photograph reproduced with permission of Bob Willingham.

Every effort has been made to contact copyright holders of any material reproduced in this book. Any omissions will be rectified in subsequent printings if notice is given to the publishers.

Contents

Japanese judo terms printed in italics, *like these*, are explained on page 45.

The techniques in this book are described as they would be performed by a right-sided fighter. Many fighters, though, are left-sided, and they would perform the same techniques by twisting to the right, for example, rather than the left.

An Olympic final

Sydney, Australia, September 22, 2000—the Olympic judo competition was drawing to a close, but the arena was still packed with spectators. They were waiting for one of the most eagerly anticipated contests of the games. The final of the men's heavyweight competition was about to begin. On one side was France's David Douillet and on the other, Japan's Shinichi Shinohara.

A clash of two giants

Douillet had already won two Olympic medals—a bronze in Barcelona, Spain, in 1992 and then a gold in Atlanta in 1996. Shortly after Atlanta, Douillet was involved in a serious motorcycle accident. He recovered from his injuries to return to competition and win the 1997 World Championships, beating Shinohara in the final. The win was controversial, as it came from a penalty given against Shinohara by a French judge. Controversy was to haunt the 2000 Olympic final, too.

In 1999, a back injury stopped Douillet from taking part in the World Championships. At these championships, Shinohara won ten of his eleven fights by *ippon*—a decisive score—and took both the heavyweight and open crowns. The stage was set for a clash between two giants of the judo world.

Ninety seconds into the 2000 Olympic final Douillet launched an attack, trying to throw Shinohara. But Shinohara twisted away from the throw—both fighters hit the mat, Douillet landing on his back. The referee raised his arm to indicate a minor score, *yuko*, for Douillet. The crowd looked to the judges. One seemed to indicate that Shinohara had won by *ippon*. The other seemed to agree with the referee. Finally, Douillet was awarded *yuko*.

In the end, only this minor score separated the two fighters. The Japanese team manager (Yasuhiro Yamashita, a judo legend who had won gold at the 1984 Los Angeles Games) launched a protest.

Shinohara throws an opponent during the 1997 World Championships. That year, he lost in the final to Douillet.

But the result stood. Douillet managed to win a second gold and then retired from international judo competition. Shinohara was crushed and cried throughout the medal ceremony.

A controversial ending

The decision in this bout was a close one, and the judges at the side of the mat did not have the advantage of endless TV replays. Most people now agree that neither fighter should have been awarded a score. But no matter how controversial, all judo fighters have to live with the decision of the judges.

Douillet and Shinohara (wearing blue) during their fight at the 2000 Olympics.

Olympic judo fact

Until David Douillet's victory in 2000, no fighter had ever won judo medals at three different Olympics.

Douillet raises his arms in triumph after taking gold at Sydney while, to the right, Shinohara looks distraught.

The roots of judo

Judo grew out of a Japanese fighting style called ju-jitsu. Ju-jitsu includes techniques that use short weapons—stabbing and slashing, for example—as well as weaponless techniques such as hitting, kicking, and choking. Ju-jitsu was adapted by a person named Jigoro Kano, who founded the fighting style called Kodokan Judo.

Shown above is one of the few photos of Jigoro Kano, who invented judo in 1882. His sport has since spread around the whole world.

Early competition

The first *dojo*—a judo practice area—had nine students, but the sport grew rapidly. In 1886 the Tokyo police held a match between Kodokan Judo fighters and one of the most famous ju-jitsu schools, the Totsuka. The Kodokan Judo fighters tied two fights and won the other thirteen. By 1888, judo had been adopted as the official self-defense system for the Tokyo police.

Judo in the Olympics

Judo's popularity spread throughout the 1900s. In 1964 the Olympics were held in Tokyo, and judo medals were awarded for the first time. Back then there were three weight categories—light, middle, and heavyweight—and competition was open only to men. Women's judo first appeared at the Olympics in Seoul, South Korea, in 1988. It was a demonstration sport at those games. In 1992 women's medals were awarded for the first time, and women's judo has been a part of the games ever since.

Here Anton Geesink of the Netherlands is pictured defeating Koji Sone of Japan, to win gold at the 1961 World Championships in the men's open division. Geesink was the first non-Japanese judoka to win a title and went on to take gold at the 1964 Olympics in Rome, Italy.

The spirit of judo

Judo is sometimes known as the gentle way, although to anyone who has just been on the wrong end of a winning throw, it feels anything but gentle. It got this name because judo is based on the idea of using an opponent's force against him or her, which is more "gentle" than using your own power alone. Judo has its own character, which is very different from football or basketball, for example, where players may sometimes argue with referees and coaches. Judo students must listen carefully to their instructors and try hard to follow their advice. Above all, every *judoka* is expected to show the sport as a whole—including other fighters, coaches, judges, and officials—complete respect.

Great Britain's Sharon Rendle (left) *performs a shoulder throw at the World Championships in Paris, France, in 1997.*

"Traditional" versus "wrestling" styles

Today, two main styles of judo exist. The first is the "traditional" style, which has developed from the techniques of Jigoro Kano. It is reasonably upright and uses gripping on the opponent's jacket as an important part of the technique. The second style, developed in countries that were formerly part of the Soviet Union, is sometimes called the Russian or wrestling style. This developed partly from traditional wrestling techniques, but it uses jacket grips far less. Some wrestling-style fighters even train without wearing their jacket.

Champion fact

The first-ever women's world judo champion was Great Britain's Jane Bridge in 1980. She fought in the under-48 kg category.

Getting started

Many people start to learn judo when they are at school. They join a small club that meets once or twice a week to practice. The club also sends fighters to competitions and grades him or her on the different levels of judo. Once the fighter becomes more interested in the sport and wants more practice, he or she may join a bigger club with better training facilities and higher level coaching.

Clothing and equipment

Judo gear is relatively simple. The full judo outfit is known as *gi*. For male fighters it is made up of a jacket and pants made of strong cotton or a similar fabric. It also has a strong belt that ties around the outside of the jacket. The belt's color and markings show what grade the fighter has reached. Female fighters also wear a white leotard or T-shirt. The T-shirt must be tucked into their pants. No shoes are worn.

The other main piece of equipment is the *tatami*—the mat on which practice and competition take place. The *tatami* is used to limit the fighting area and to cushion the impact of falling. In competitions it must be at least 26 square feet (8 square meters), with a 3.3-foot (1 meter) danger area and a 9.8-foot (3 meters) safety zone outside it. However, smaller *tatami* are used for practice.

Temporary and permanent *dojos*

Many smaller judo clubs have their *dojo* in a space they share with other groups—a school gym or community center, for example. This means that after each session the *tatami* must be cleared away and the space left free for others to use. As judo grows in popularity, however, there are increasing numbers of permanent *dojo*, where practice space is available all the time. These *dojo* often have highly experienced teachers, who are often top-level fighters able to teach promising young people.

These young judo students are learning their first throws as their coach stands in the background, checking that everything is being done correctly.

Training groups

At the *dojo*, people practice together in groups of up to twenty, with one teacher explaining and watching what they do. Every fighter works with a training partner. First, the person practices the technique he or she is learning. Then that person becomes an opponent for the other person on which to practice. It is important that everyone treats their training partner with respect, because without them it would not be possible to learn.

This group of judo students is watching a demonstration of a new technique. Afterwards, they will split into pairs to practice the move—first one letting himself be thrown, then the other.

Safety fact

Judo belts must always be knotted at the front, to prevent injuries to the spine caused by falling on the knot.

How to tie a judo belt

Judo belts have to be tied in a specific way:
1) Place the very middle of the belt on your stomach. Loop both ends behind you and bring them back to the front.
2) Cross the right end over the left end, then thread it up and under both loops, in the middle of your stomach.
3) Cross the left end over the right end and tie them tightly together. Both ends should be equal length.

Judo structure

When beginners join a judo club, they get a license and membership in their national judo organization. The license allows them to take part in exams to move up judo levels and to enter competitions. Fighters who have only just started to learn judo wear a white belt. As they become more skilled, they earn different colored belts by taking examinations (pages 40–41).

Judo ranks

The color of belt that junior fighters are allowed to wear varies from country to country. In many places, juniors have eighteen grades, called *mon*. The belt order is white, yellow, orange, green, blue, and brown. Each belt can have one, two, or three red bars sewn onto it—three bars is a higher *mon* than one.

Seniors (usually aged sixteen and over) have ten grades, called *kyu*. Reaching the tenth *kyu* allows you to wear a black belt. The tenth *kyu* is divided into ten further grades, called *dan*. First to fifth *dan* fighters wear a black belt, which they can wear through to tenth *dan*. However, if they choose to, they can instead wear a red-and-white blocked belt from sixth to eighth *dan*, and a red belt at ninth or tenth *dan*.

Scoring in competitions

In competition, fighters win—or advance to the next round—in one of three ways. Scoring either a single *ippon* or two *waza-ari* (page 11) will win the contest outright. If neither fighter manages this, points are added up from the *waza-ari*, *yuko* and *koka* each fighter has scored. One *waza-ari* beats all *yuko*, and one *yuko* beats all *koka*. So no fighter can lose to an opponent who has scored lots of points, but at a lower grade.

Here, a groundwork technique is being demonstrated to a group of students. Watching a more experienced, higher-ranked judo fighter is the first step in learning new skills.

The judge signals a yuko *score* to one of the fighters in this contest. Unless ippon *has been scored, ending the contest, they will return to their starting positions on the* tatami (mat) *and get to grips again.*

Judo scoring categories

The judges indicate scores in the bout using a system of colored flags. Usually there is a referee on the *tatami* with the fighters, plus two other judges nearby. There are four different categories of score in judo competition:

Ippon
i) a throw where the opponent lands with force on his or her back
ii) submission from an armlock or stranglehold
iii) a 25-second hold-down

Waza-ari
i) a throw where the opponent lands with force, partly on his or her side
ii) a 21- to 25-second hold-down

Yuko
i) a throw lacking force or where the opponent lands on his or her side
ii) a 15- to 20-second hold-down

Koka
i) a throw where the opponent lands on his or her thigh or buttocks
ii) a 10- to 15-second hold-down.

Weight divisions fact

At senior level, men and women each fight in one of seven possible weight divisions, as listed in the table below. There is also an open division in which fighters of different weights can compete against each other.

Senior men judo weight divisions						
under 60 kg (132 lbs)	60–66 kg (132–146 lbs)	66–73 kg (146–161 lbs)	73–81 kg (161–179 lbs)	81–90 kg (179–198 lbs)	90–100 kg (198–220 lbs)	over 100 kg (220 lbs)
Senior women judo weight divisions						
under 48 kg (106 lbs)	48–52 kg (106–115 lbs)	52–57 kg (115–127 lbs)	57–63 kg (127–139 lbs)	63–70 kg (139–154 lbs)	70–78 kg (154–172 lbs)	over 78 kg (172 lbs)

Falling

Falling is the first skill a new *judoka*—the name for a person who practices judo—learns. It is also an important skill for competitors at the very top level. Skill at falling can mean the difference between suffering *ippon* and losing, or *yuko,* and staying in the fight. But the main reason all *judokas* need to develop skill at falling is that it helps prevent injuries when being thrown.

Protection

The most important parts of the body to protect against injury are the head, neck, and base of the spine. Falling techniques, which are known as *ukemi*, have been developed to help shield these areas from injury as much as possible. Continuous practice of *ukemi* also strengthens a *judoka's* muscles, making it harder for his or her body to be injured.

Protection from injury is also one of the reasons why *judoka* fight in weight categories. Fighting people of a similar weight makes it less likely that someone will be dangerously overpowered by his or her opponent.

Falling essentials

The basic skills of falling are to keep your head tucked in and your back bent forwards. *Judoka* use his or her hands, arms, feet, and legs to cushion the impact of the fall, rather than taking the full force of it on any one part of the body and thus suffering an injury. These falling techniques are also known as break-falls.

These fighters will hit the mat with a lot of force. Using proper technique to break their fall is crucial if they want to avoid being injured. For this reason, break-falls are the first thing a new judoka *learns when beginning the sport.*

Training benefits

As well as making it harder for an opponent to score points, mastering *ukemi* can also build a *judoka's* confidence, because he or she would be less afraid of being thrown. This in turn makes the *judoka* more confident about launching attacks in practice sessions, which has a benefit for competitions. *Judoka* can experiment with new throws and techniques in practice, then apply them in competition.

Different types of *ukemi*

Various techniques are used for falling, depending on the direction of the fall. To the back or side, the palms of the hands, the forearms—for side falls—and the outer thigh are used to cushion the *judoka's* body. In front falls, the knees, forearms, and palms are used. These are also used to cushion the fall when a *judoka* spins out sideways.

In a forward break-fall, *judoka* roll forwards onto one shoulder and then the opposite hip. His or her legs come over practically straight, ideally with enough force to allow the fighter to continue the roll back to a standing position.

This judoka *is executing a backwards break-fall, using his hands and forearms to take some of the force of the landing.*

Ukemi fact

A good way for a *judoka* to keep his or her head tucked in properly is to look straight at the knot of the belt.

This forward break-fall technique is an excellent way to avoid injury. The force of the fall is absorbed in the roll forwards, and often the judoka *can stand straight up again afterwards.*

The basics

Top-level judo players all need to have excellent balance, especially the ability to keep their feet rooted to the floor even when being pushed and shoved by an opponent. The big throws that make judo such a spectacular sport are the result of one fighter breaking another's balance. It is skill at this ability, rather than power, that usually decides a contest between fighters of the same weight.

Six basic postures

There are six basic postures in judo, each of which is designed to allow a fighter to shift his or her body position without losing his or her balance.

These postures are:
- natural posture—standing relaxed and upright with feet shoulder width apart
- right and left natural posture—standing relaxed and upright but with either the right or left foot forward
- defensive posture—body upright, but feet slightly more than shoulder-width apart and knees slightly bent
- right and left defensive posture—similar to above, but with either the right or left foot forward

The judoka *on the right has adopted the right defensive posture.*

Basics fact

Right from the start, a *judoka* should concentrate on mastering the basic skills of judo correctly. If he or she is lazy about getting them right at first, every subsequent practice session using the wrong techniques makes it a little bit harder to get them right in the future.

Djamel Bouras of France (wearing the red belt) *tries to take hold of K. Savchis of Russia during a bout at the 1996 Atlanta Olympics.*

Taking hold

Another main element of a top *judoka's* skills is taking hold of his or her opponent. This is known as *kumikata*. The *judoka* grips either his or her opponent's body or, more usually, the *gi*—clothing—which can then be used to try and force the opponent off balance. Normally, he or she grips a combination of sleeves, the side of the jacket, and the lapel. Some *judoka* are known for vise-like grips—one of the best ever at this technique was Britain's Olympic silver medalist Neil Adams.

Top *judoka*, such as Kosei Inoue of Japan, practice his or her throwing techniques again and again, using various different holding positions. In a high-level contest, there may be only one chance for him or her to take a good grip of the opponent, so the judo player practices throws from a variety of different starting points.

Neil Adams *(facing the camera) was one of Britain's top* judoka *in the 1980s. Here he is pictured fighting for a grip on an opponent. Adams's viselike grip was famous throughout the judo world.*

Tai sabaki

Tai sabaki is the name given to shifting your body position to stop your opponent from throwing you. By anticipating an attack, top *judoka* can block it using *tai sabaki*, adapting his or her body position and balance to make the throw impossible. It is also possible to move with the momentum of an attack, meaning that the opponent cannot get enough leverage into the throw to finish it successfully.

Throws

Just as keeping your balance is an essential defensive skill for all *judoka*, breaking an opponent's balance is a crucial attacking skill. Throwing techniques revolve around catching or forcing an opponent off-balance. A *judoka* also often uses an opponent's own momentum against him or her. Top *judoka* make their throws with great speed and decisiveness.

Kuzushi—breaking balance

Breaking an opponent's balance is known as *kuzushi*. Making a throw in judo depends on a combination of factors. To be successful, an attacker must have good balance and body position, and a strong and well-positioned grip on his or her opponent. Only then can balance be broken in the correct way to allow a throw to be made successfully.

Different grips on an opponent can be used to break her or his balance in different ways. Breaking an opponent's balance backwards might make the person vulnerable to *ouchi gari*, a throw that would continue the backwards motion. Breaking it to the right might make the person vulnerable to *uchimata*, which begins with the opponent moving to the side and down.

Hip throws

Many judo throwing techniques are based on the large hip throw, otherwise known as *ogoshi*. This throw uses the attacker's hips and legs to throw the opponent. The attacker turns inside the defender's grip with slightly bent knees, pulling on the sleeve and the back of the belt. As the attacker straightens his or her knees, the opponent is lifted and rolled over the attacker's hip, then deposited on his or her back on the floor.

Here, British judoka Michelle Rogers is using a classic hip throw, uki goshi*, to try for an* ippon *score at a tournament in Paris in 2001. Rogers sensed that her opponent's balance was weak and reacted quickly. The photo also shows how important it is to have a good grip.*

Shoulder throws

Shoulder throws are often even more spectacular than hip throws. The attacker has to get down low to throw her or his opponent, and the throw often takes power from the strength of the attacker's bent legs.

In *morote seoi nage*—the two-handed shoulder throw, for example—fighters grip the opponent's right sleeve and left lapel. The attacker pulls on the right sleeve, turning his or her hand so that the little finger is on top, then steps inside and across with the right foot. The attacker's elbow slips inside, too, under the opponent's right armpit. The aim is to end up with bent knees and the opponent's chest locked against your back. The attacker's left hand continues to pull, and the opponent is thrown over the right shoulder.

Kosei Inoue of Japan takes gold in the 2000 Olympics. He scored ippon for this throw of Nicolas Gill from Canada. The photo clearly shows how the leverage points of lapel, sleeve, and calf have been used to completely break Gill's balance.

Kuzushi fact

Although photos often show *kuzushi* techniques with the opponent standing still, they are only properly effective when the opponent is moving.

Reaping and sweeping

Top *judokas* can attack their opponents in many ways—with a variety of techniques. Among them are reaping and sweeping throws, where the opponents find their feet disappearing out from under them, swept away by an unexpected attack. These often use the legs and feet, but for some reaps attackers may use their hands. Each reap, as with other throws, depends on specific *kuzushi* balance-breaking techniques to make it successful. The leg movements alone will not work.

In this photo, Darcel Yandzi of France can be seen throwing Bronislaw Wolkowicz of Poland with osoto gari, *the large outer reap.*

Large reaps

Large reaps are performed using the leg to sweep opponents off their feet. The first main type is the large outer reap (*osoto gari*), where attackers step inside and use their right leg to sweep away an opponent's right leg, forcing him or her to fall to the attacker's left.

For the large inner reap (*ouchi gari*), the attacker steps forward and hooks her or his right leg around the opponent's left leg. By staying balanced, the attacker is able to lift the opponent's right leg forward. The opponent is then thrown to the ground.

Kosoto gari, *the small outer reap, is caught perfectly by the camera in this photo. Slightly off-balance, the fighter facing the camera has had her left foot swept out from beneath her. With her feet so far apart, and one foot in the air, she cannot avoid being thrown.*

Small reaps

Small reaps are those in which attackers use their foot, rather than leg, to unbalance their opponent. In the small outer reap (*kosoto gari*), the attacker's left leg steps behind the defender's right, then sweeps it forwards so that the defender falls over backwards and to the left. In the small inner reap (*kouchi gari*), attackers use their right foot to sweep the opponent's right foot out and to the right.

Hips and thighs

Other throws use the hips—for example, the hip wheel *koshi guruma* and the hip sweep *harai goshi*—or the thigh—for example, the inner thigh reaping throw *uchimata*.

Technique fact

The position of the head is crucial in throwing technique. The head determines the direction of the throw, so *judokas* look in the direction they want the throw to go.

Foul fact

Kicking is not allowed in judo, so it is important for all *judoka* to learn the reaping and sweeping techniques well. Otherwise he or she risks being given a foul by the referee.

Using the hands

Use of the hands on an opponent's legs is popular with *judoka* who use the wrestling style (page 7). One popular example of this is the two-handed reap (*morote gari*). In this move, as the opponent tries to take hold, the attacker steps forward and grabs the backs of the opponent's legs. Pushing the right shoulder into the knot of the defender's belt, the attacker lifts the legs. The opponent is thrown to the floor. This throw has to be made quickly or the defender can twist out of it, since the attacker has no control over their upper body.

Kellie Roberts of Great Britain attacks with kouchi gari, *the small inner reap. Roberts has stepped inside to sweep away her opponent's right foot with her own left foot. The other fighter clings on, hoping to avoid ippon.*

Advanced technique

Once *judokas* have mastered the basic techniques, they are ready to use them in combination and to adapt their attacks according to what their opponent is doing. It is this ability to make endless adaptations during a match, often instinctively, which is a hallmark of the best judo stars.

Combinations

When fighting an experienced opponent, one simple attack is unlikely to be successful. Top *judokas* are able to recognize an attack as it begins and can shift their body weight to block it. Sometimes an attacker can use this blocking movement as the start of a new attack, making it possible for them to throw the defender in a different way. This is known as a combination. The best competitors may perform several feints until they feel they have broken an opponent's balance and can launch a true attacking move. Sometimes the new attack is in the same direction as the feint—this is called *renzoku waza*. When the new attack takes a new direction, it is called *renraku waza*.

An attempted attack by El Salvador's Ledis Salazar (white) has failed, leaving her off-balance. Karina Bryant of Great Britain (blue) takes instant advantage, using the momentum of the attack to throw her opponent to the floor.

Counters

In competition judo, the rules say that both fighters must have an attacking attitude. Those who are seen as too defensive risk being penalized by the referee. But this does not mean that they must both launch new attacks during the entire contest. One of the key techniques in judo is to use the movement from your opponent's attack to launch your own counterattack, or counter. The attacker will have had to shift his or her weight to attack, making it possible for her or his balance to be broken more easily.

Practice fact

The best way to develop competition skills is in a free-practice session, known as *randori*. This is where *judokas* split into pairs for mini-bouts in which they can attempt combinations and counters, among other things. There is no referee so they must work together, under the eyes of their coach.

Ryoko Tamura and "Yawara!"

Ryoko Tamura is a legendary figure in Japan. She has even had a comic strip, "Yawara," modeled after her. Despite being tiny, even for the under-48 kg division, she has won five world titles. After two Olympic silver medals (in 1992 and 1996), she finally won gold at the Sydney Olympics in 2000. Tamura is famous for being incredibly quick, which often catches her opponents off-guard.

Sacrifices

Sacrifices are when *judokas* appear to allow themselves to be put in a weak position, only to turn it to their own advantage. Usually this means that they go down on their back or side in order to throw their opponent using their feet and body movement. This is fun for beginners to practice and is very dramatic, like something out of an action film. But against experienced opponents, sacrifices are risky unless they are done extremely well, because the person performing them starts from a position of disadvantage.

Sacrifices are most commonly used by wrestling-style fighters—their style of judo makes them more naturally comfortable fighting on the *tatami*. The contrast of styles when a traditional fighter meets a wrestling fighter can make for interesting tactics from both sides.

Groundwork

Although not as spectacular to untrained observers as throws, groundwork is equally important. Top-level competitors such as Great Britain's John Buchanan have to be as strong at groundwork as everything else. This can give them the confidence to attempt throws, since they know that if the throw is unsuccessful or only partially successful, they will be able to continue the attack on the ground.

The fighter on top in this photo is employing kesa gatame, *also known as the scarf hold because the opponent's neck is wrapped up like a scarf.*

Throws to holds

The best *judoka* are able to make some throws with the possible aim of turning them into a hold on the ground. This means that even if the throw does not score *ippon*, it can still lead to a strong groundwork position and the possibility of more points or victory. This change is called transition.

Hold-downs

Hold-downs—called *osaekomi waza*—are techniques where the opponent is pinned to the ground, usually on his or her back. Referees announce *osaekomi* when they think the following have happened:

• The attacker has his or her body in one of two approved positions.
• The defender is under the control of the attacker and has one or both shoulders plus the back in contact with the mat.
• The attacker's legs or body are not controlled by the defender's legs.
• At least one of the contestants has part of his or her body within the competition area.

Once the referee has called *osaekomi*, the countdown begins. If the hold remains in place for 25 seconds, *ippon* is scored and the contest is over.

The fighter on top here has wrapped up his opponent in yoko shiho gatame, *otherwise known as the side-locking, four-corner hold.*

Armlocks

Top *judoka* will sometimes be able to fight back from a hold-down using an armlock. Armlocks—*kansetsu waza*—are techniques in which pressure is put on an opponent's elbow joint in order to force a submission. There are other *kansetsu waza* in judo, but only those applied to the elbow are allowed in competition.

Groundwork points

Groundwork is important because it can win a contest or extra points.

- A 25-second hold-down wins the contest with *ippon*.
- A 21- to 25-second hold-down scores *waza-ari*.
- A 15- to 20-second hold-down scores *yuko*.

Bridging fact

Bridging is one of the most common escapes from a hold. Using mainly leg and back muscles, as well as arms, *judokas* lift their hips off the floor. The effect is to roll their attacker off or push them away. At the very least, they can stop their back from being in contact with the ground, breaking the hold temporarily.

Warming up and stretching

In judo even a world-class *judoka* is likely to find his or her body being bent out of shape and subjected to very unusual stresses and strains. This makes the warming-up process even more important than in most sports. *Judoka* also find flexibility helpful, as it allows them to twist their bodies with greater ease.

Warming up

Warming up properly before starting hard judo practice or competition is crucial. It is important to warm up progressively, starting relatively slowly. Judo coaches make sure their *judoka* warm up four main categories of muscles—the legs; the abdominal belt; the shoulders, chest, and arms; and the upper back and neck.

A few useful warm-up stretches are explained on the right, but there are many more. *Judokas* should never perform a stretch unless they have seen it demonstrated and know how to do it properly. They should never keep a stretch going until it hurts, as this risks injury. Instead, they should just hold it at the moment when it becomes slightly uncomfortable, then breathe deeply from the stomach to relax.

- Thigh stretch—this is done standing, keeping the hips level and pulling the heel of one foot up to the bottom. The exercise is then repeated with the other foot.

- Back/shoulder stretch—the elbow of one arm is pulled up behind the head, so that the forearm points down the spine. This is then repeated with the other arm.

- Side stretches—the *judoka* stands with his or her feet just over shoulder-width apart and one hand on a hip. He or she then bends to that side, stretching the other arm over the head, leaning to the side.

- Neck rolls—the head is tipped to the left, then rolled down so the chin is on the chest, then tipped back up to the right. This is then repeated in the opposite direction. The head should *never* be rolled backwards.

Ryoko Tamura of Japan stretches during a training session at the 2000 Sydney Olympics.

Flexibility is vital if a judoka is to avoid being held down and losing points during competition.

Craig Fallon

One fighter famous for using his flexibility to escape from dangerous situations is the young British *judoka* Craig Fallon *(pictured in blue)*. In 2002 Fallon won the gold at the Commonwealth Games. But one of his greatest successes—one that put him third in the European rankings—came at a tournament in Paris in 2003. There, Fallon managed to escape from an *uchimata* throw by his South Korean opponent in the match's first exchange, twisting through the air and landing on his feet. Had the throw been successful, the match would have been lost. As it was, Fallon survived and went on to win one of judo's most prestigious gold medals.

Flexibility

Increased flexibility is helpful for almost all athletes. To develop this, they need to follow a regular routine of stretching exercises—ideally daily—in order to make sure their muscles are loose. This is because loose muscles allow limbs to move more freely than would otherwise be the case. *Judokas* find that flexibility of their neck, back, shoulder, waist, and hip muscles helps them develop their techniques.

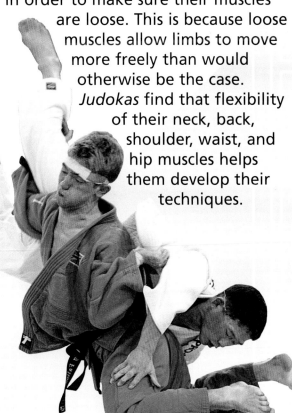

Physical conditioning

Like all world-class athletes, international-standard *judoka* need to be extremely fit. A match lasts five minutes, which may not sound very long but these are five minutes in which a lot of very concentrated activity takes place. In addition, a *judoka* has to go through up to six bouts in a few hours to reach the championship. Finally, the need for fitness is even greater in competitions known as *kohaku*, in which the winner stays on the mat until defeated.

This illustration shows the most important muscle groups used in judo. World-class fighters need to be in great shape overall, however.

Using different muscles

Judo uses four main groups of muscles:

- the abdominal belt
- the upper back and neck
- the shoulders, chest, and arms
- the legs

As well as building fitness, *judokas* aim to build power in these areas. They also aim to increase their muscle reaction time, to allow faster techniques.

Bodyweight training

Most young *judokas* are asked by their coaches not to use weights until their bodies have finished growing. Using weights before then can lead to serious injury—sometimes long-term—as muscles build up too much power for the bones growing around them. Instead, coaches encourage the use of body-weight training—sit-ups, push-ups, squat thrusts, etc. This also provides excellent training for top *judokas*.

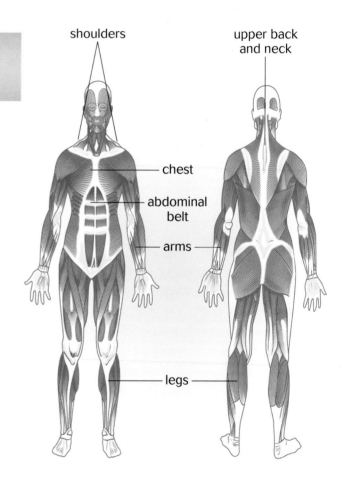

shoulders

upper back and neck

chest

abdominal belt

arms

legs

Weight training

Later on in their careers, many *judoka* use weight training to develop power and stamina. Some use free weights, but the majority today use multi-gym machines, since the risk of injury on these is usually far less than with free weights.

Sit-ups are a good way for young judokas *to exercise without damaging their bodies.*

Increasing reaction times

The best way of increasing the speed with which a technique can be used is repetition. Top *judoka* may practice a particular move several hundred times a day, every day, as a way of programming the muscles to repeat the move automatically.

The role of a team physiotherapist

Top *judokas* are accompanied to many of their international contests by a physiotherapist. The physiotherapist's jobs include:

- Checking that the whole team is healthy before they leave for the competition and that no one has an injury that will stop them fighting.
- Assessing and, if possible, treating injuries that happen in competition. Serious injuries mean a fighter must withdraw, but minor injuries to fingers, for example, can be taped up.

Injury fact

Most injuries from judo are to joints, caused by the twists and strains of practice and competition. Fingers, wrists, elbows, shoulders, knees, toes, and ankles can all be affected. The first stage in treating most of these injuries is usually a regime known as PRICE. This stands for:

- **P**revent the injured *judoka* from moving
- **R**est the injury
- **I**ce the injury
- **C**ompress, or apply pressure to, the injured area
- **E**levate the injured limb to stop the swelling from becoming worse.

World-class training

Top *judoka* follow a punishing training schedule, which includes both getting into shape and practicing judo. They also go to special training camps where they can practice against other top fighters, sometimes from other countries. Of course, on top of all this there are regular competitions to attend, not to mention academic studies for the younger *judoka*!

Sophie Cox is a young British judoka. In 2002, she won a bronze medal at the Commonwealth Games in Manchester, England.

Sophie Cox's competition checklist

Do not forget your:
- blue and white *gi*
- white T-shirts
- water and high-energy drink
- energy bars, chocolate, and blueberry muffins

Cox thinks it is important to have high-energy foods handy for competition days.
- warm clothes for between fights.

Training fact

Many top *judoka* train 3.5 or 4 hours a day, 6 days a week. That is around 100 hours a month, or 1,200 hours a year. Put another way, that is around 50 days and nights of the year spent in training!

Diary of an international judoka

In 2003, Sophie Cox was a young international *judoka* who fought in the under-57 kg weight division. Prior to the 2004 Olympics, she was a student at the Bisham Abbey National Judo Academy in Great Britain. As well as practicing judo, she was also studying for a degree in Health and Exercise. Cox's diary of the first three months of 2003 give a good idea of what life is like for an international *judoka*.

January 2003

January 3—international training camp held in Great Britain. Day starts at 6:20 A.M., with a groundwork session at 7:00. Breakfast, then a technique session at 10:00. After this, running at 1:00 P.M., followed by a log-carry race through the woods. Back on the mat by 7:30 P.M. for more judo until 9:30, then off to home and to bed!

January 7–12—training camp in Munich, Germany.

January 24–26—tournament in Moscow, Russia. Record: 1–1.

February 2003

February 8—tournament in Paris. Record: won in rounds one and two, lost in round three, so into the repercharge competition—from which *judoka* can win a bronze medal. Won first fight, lost second and knocked out of competition. Great that Craig Fallon, also from Great Britain, managed to win a gold, though!

February 24–27—international training camp, Hamburg, Germany. Just five sessions, but very intense, with world-class *judoka* and coaches.

March 2003

March 18—noticed a cauliflower—swollen—ear appearing, so went to doctor to have it drained.

March 22—tournament in Rotterdam, the Netherlands. First fight won by *ippon* but slight abdominal muscle strain in the process. Second fight won. Third fight won, but armlock by opponent causes slight injury. Semi-final against current world champion from Cuba, Luputey. Score is even at end of five minutes, so into "golden score" overtime. A passivity penalty—a score given to Luputey because I was not aggressive enough—wins the contest for her. Into contest for bronze medal and won it!

Cox was then picked for the European Championships and won another bronze medal. She, like many other promising young *judoka*, would then set her sights on qualifying for the Olympics.

Learning new techniques

Experienced coaches and *judokas* can spot a skilled fighter quickly. Such a fighter will show economy of movement and correct application of power. Their technique will demonstrate exactly what Jigoro Kano, the founder of judo, meant when he spoke of "maximum efficiency" or "best use of energy."

Keeping balance in a match is at the heart of successful judo. Here, the fighter in blue retains good balance, while the white is vulnerable to attack.

Repetition fact

Top competitors say that practice makes permanent—not perfect! They mean that if a skill is not learned correctly from the start, it will not work perfectly, no matter how much it is practiced.

Learning new moves

Coaches try to develop skilled technique in their *judoka* through an understanding of how humans learn new movements. As a demonstration of what this means, think about learning to walk. No baby is ever born able to walk: his or her muscles are not strong enough, and the baby lacks the physical skill and balance. Yet, within a year and a half most children can walk. There are three key elements in how they learn.

1) They see other people walking. This makes a baby understand that walking is possible and also gives them an image of what they are trying to learn.

2) They start trying to walk themselves. Their muscles lack strength, and their brains do not know how to coordinate the tricky combination of movement and balance, which they sense through their eyes and inner ear. Through repeated attempts, they steadily develop this sense.

3) Finally, babies are able to take their first few steps. The first ones are wobbly, but every day their muscle memory and strength increase. Finally they are able to walk without thinking about it.

Judoka learn new skills in a very similar way to babies learning to walk, and for exactly the same reasons.

Stage 1—demonstration

First, *judoka* see a new skill being demonstrated by someone who is experienced in it. Often the demonstration begins in slow motion, before building up to full speed. This gives the *judoka* a mental picture of how the skill is performed.

Stage 2—coached movement

Next, *judokas* themselves attempt the skill. At first, their muscles are not used to the movement, and their brain has to exercise conscious control over each step. At this stage a good coach is crucial, as he or she can adjust the *judoka's* body position and movement until it is perfect.

Only through repeating moves again and again in practice do judoka *learn to do them without thinking in competition.*

Demonstrating techniques to junior judoka is one of the ways in which senior fighters pass on their skills. The next step for the juniors is to work on the technique under the guidance of their coach.

Stage 3—repetition

Once the skill has been learned correctly, the *judoka* must build up muscle memory, so that it can be used by reflex in competition. This comes from repeated practice, doing the same movement perhaps hundreds of times a day until it becomes as automatic as walking.

Timing fact

Timing is crucial in judo—even the most skilled fighter will not be successful with an attack, if it is not timed as their opponent is off balance. This is why *randori*—free practice—is so important. It allows *judoka* to develop an instinct for which skills work best in different circumstances.

Eating for fitness

In some ways, a *judoka's* body is like a machine. The demands of world-class competitions such as the Olympics and World Championships are very high. A *judoka* has to be able to perform complicated movements again and again, with a minimum loss of efficiency in the course of several bouts. And, just like a machine, a *judoka* runs better if he or she is filled with the right fuel—healthy food.

What food does

The food we eat does one or more of three jobs. It provides materials for building, repairing or maintaining body tissues. It helps regulate body processes such as digestion. And it serves as fuel to provide energy, which the body needs to maintain all its functions.

Balanced diet

For top *judokas*, who put their bodies under great stress, eating enough of the right types of food is even more important than for normal people. Many top fighters take advice from nutritionists—experts in how the food we eat affects us—to make sure that the food they eat includes enough of the various different types (see panel on the right).

A healthy meal is an essential part of any athlete's preparation for competition.

Food fact

Nutritionists recommend a diet using a proportion of food from each of these five groups:

- breads, cereals, rice, and pasta
- vegetables
- fruits
- milk, yogurt, and cheese
- meat, poultry, fish, dried beans and peas, eggs, and nuts

Fats are also essential but, like sweets, should be eaten in small quantities.

Sweating down

Judoka fight in weight categories— for example, "under-60 kg." This means that some fighters are right on the limit of the category—for instance, someone who weighs 62 kg. People have been known to try to "sweat down" to a lower category by running, swimming, or even going into a sauna, to sweat out fluid and reduce their weight. They do this in an attempt to be a bigger fighter in a smaller weight category. But sweating down is a very dangerous. Water is probably the body's most crucial nutrient. Suddenly losing then regaining significant amounts of water can cause serious damage, as well as weakening the body's muscles and reaction times.

Competition day

On competition day, most *judokas* prefer to eat a light meal several hours before their bouts begin. It is best to avoid fats and meat, which break down slowly in the stomach and will still be being digested hours later. They may "top off" their energy levels with a snack or, even better, an energy drink that will help their body replace lost nutrients.

Banned drugs fact

There are two main types of banned drugs that could be used by judo players who want to break the rules. These are:

- anabolic steroids, which increase muscle bulk and power and can make people more aggressive.
- stimulants, which increase reaction times and, in some circumstances, aggression.

Top *judoka*, like many other athletes, are subject to tests at competitions and in training to make sure they are not using banned drugs.

Judoka *who use anabolic steroids like this risk being caught and banned from entering competitions.*

100 Tablets

Dianabol®

BIO DELTA
FARMACÊUTICA

TABOL
Comprimidos

Methandrostenolone
5mg

5 mg
Comprimido
Por Via Oral

DELTA FARMACÊUTICA
LNBOA, RAU DE SANTIAGO
LISBOA

Competition

High-level judo competitions all follow a similar format. The fighters weigh in, to make sure they are the right weight for the category they have entered. Then there is a short break before the bouts begin. Usually, the competition for each weight division is run from start to finish in a single day, so the champion is crowned that evening.

Weighing in

The weigh-in normally begins early in the morning, at about 7:30 A.M. The fighters are allowed about an hour of "unofficial" weigh-in, to check their weight without it being recorded. Once the official weigh-in begins, however, fighters are only allowed on the scales once—as soon as they step off, their weight is recorded. Occasionally, fighters who have come in a little over their weight division have had to shed clothes while standing on the scales. They do this to knock off a tiny bit of weight before the official recording is made.

Team managers

Once the competition gets under way, the team manager makes sure the *judokas* know when they are fighting and that they are ready on time. This helps the competitors to focus on the match ahead of them, instead of other details.

Japan's Shinichi Shinohara looks out across the competition floor towards the crowd as he prepares to do battle with an opponent.

Weigh-in fact

At the Atlanta Olympics in 1996, David Khakaleshvili, the 1992 heavyweight champion, failed to reach the venue for the weigh-in. The driver of his bus got lost, and Khakaleshvili ended up in the wrong place. Having missed the weigh-in, he was unable to defend his title—even though there is no upper weight limit on heavyweight fighters.

Warm-up areas

Competitors are not usually allowed to practice in the competition area, even days before the event begins. A separate area is set aside for them in which to warm up and to practice. This is normally where *judokas* wait for their next bout. At world-class competitions such as the Olympics and World Championships, these warm-up areas have TV screens on which *judokas* can watch the bouts that are going on as they wait. This can be a good way to discover the favorite moves of the *judoka* they may be fighting in the next round!

Competition structure

To win a tournament a *judoka* has to win all his or her bouts. But losers can still come back into the competition if the person they lost to makes it to the semi-final. This allows them to join the contest for third place and a bronze medal.

Showing respect

Respect for your opponent is an important part of judo—that is why competitors bow to each other after a match. There was controversy at the 2003 World Championships in Japan, however, as several competitors were reprimanded by officials for behavior against the rules of judo. One Egyptian *judoka* was forced to make his bow three times after being defeated, as he had not done it correctly the first or second time. Trouble also erupted *(below)* when a Japanese fighter was suspected of adding detergent to the sleeves of his *gi* to make it more slippery for his opponents to grip!

Tactics

There are a variety of factors that influence how *judokas* approach a competition. Their training, fitness, skill, previous experience, and style of fighting, for example, all have an impact on how they will perform. As well as all these factors, *judokas* must consider their tactics for a bout. Will they fight with all-out aggression like the great French *judoka* Cécile Nowak, perhaps aiming to score *ippon*? Or will they be more cautious and try to be awarded several smaller scores?

Changing tactics

As well as planning in advance, the best *judokas* are able to change their tactics to fit the circumstances of the fight. For example, a *judoka* with only a few seconds left to score *ippon* is more likely to attempt aggressive throws than a *judoka* who is leading with *waza-ari* and *yuko*. Tactics in or near the red area at the edge of the *tatami*—called the danger zone—will be different from near the center.

Attack and counterattack

Some *judokas* rely on using their own technique to move their opponent off-balance. Others wait for the opponent to move off-balance before making a crucial move. The best fighters can shift between aggression and reaction, leaving their opponent uncertain of what to expect.

Strangleholds such as this one are strictly controlled in competitive judo, because of the risk of serious injury involved in using such techniques.

Tactical variables

There are many things that can affect a *judoka's* tactics. Being confident at groundwork may mean a fighter is less worried about being thrown or making sacrifices (page 21). Once on the ground, he or she know they will have a good chance of scoring points.

Older *judokas* may use their competition experience to wait for the moment to launch a decisive attack, rather than making several feints. Someone facing an unusually aggressive fighter might decide to concentrate on keeping their balance strong and counterattacking.

The advice of a coach is important in deciding which tactics to use. Training drills are used to develop tactical ability. Coping with the fighting styles of different opponents (left- or right-handed, wrestling, defensive, offensive, etc.), fighting while behind or ahead, competing when injured or sick, and any other imaginable situations are covered in training.

Know your opponent

In world-class judo, it pays to know your opponent. In the past, Eastern European coaches in particular kept detailed files on all the *judokas* that their fighters might meet in competition. For example Neil Adams, a former international judo star from Great Britain, was amazed to find that Eastern-bloc coaches had thick files full of information about him. The researching of possible opponents—identifying their strengths, favorite throws, and weaknesses—has become more common throughout the world of top-level judo.

Cécile Nowak

Cécile Nowak of France *(right)* was known throughout her career as one of the most aggressive fighters around. In 1989 she won her first European title, and won it again in 1990, 1991, and 1992. Her first three European titles were won in final bouts against the same woman, Great Britain's Karen Briggs. The crowning moment in Nowak's career came when she defeated Ryoko Tamura of Japan (page 21) to win the 1992 Olympic gold medal.

Major competitions

Judo is a popular sport around the world, played in almost every country. This means there are always competitions going on somewhere, at some time. Most are small local tournaments. But there are some competitions that all top *judokas* have circled on their calendar, sometimes years in advance. These are the big events that top fighters hope they will one day win.

The Olympics

This is the competition all athletes want to win more than any other. Held once every four years, Olympic competitions are extremely challenging. Only the very best *judoka* win an Olympic medal of any color.

In most competitions, all fights in a particular weight division usually take place on one day. In the Olympics, however, weight divisions may be contested over two days. This gives the fighters more time to recover between bouts.

World Championships

Held in a different location every other year, the World Championships are number two on the list of all world-class *judoka*. During the championships, the top fighters in the world gather together to show who is the best.

Regional championships

Different regions also stage their own championships. For example, each year there is a European championship open only to *judoka* registered in Europe. The standard of these regional championships varies from place to place, though the championships in Asia, Europe, and North America have many world-class *judokas.*

Olympic competition is the fiercest of all. Here, the Belgian fighter Ulla Werbrouck throws Yoko Tanabe of Japan at the Atlanta Olympics in 1996.

International tournaments

There are also regular international tournaments open to top *judoka* from around the world. In Europe, for example, there are three "Super A" competitions each year—held in Moscow; Paris; and Hamburg, Germany.

The Super A tournaments are recognized as among the most competitive events in the world. Top *judoka* with Olympic- and World-Championship experience come from roughly 40 different countries to fight in the Super A contests. As well as internationally established athletes, there are always new faces on the scene hoping to prove themselves. Top British *judoka* Craig Fallon, for example, first became well known when he won at the Paris Super A in 2003.

Other A tournaments are used as qualifying tournaments, to decide whether *judoka* qualify for major international tournaments such as the Olympics.

Competition fact

Less skilled *Judokas* have several different types of competitions available to them, which will offer different levels of opponents.

- Closed competitions are only open to eligible *judoka* from clubs in a certain area.
- Invitational competitions are open only to players from clubs that have been invited to participate.
- Open competitions are open to all eligible players.
- Mini *Mon* competitions are open only to players of lower *Mon* grade, usually up to 6th *Mon* but occasionally up to 9th *Mon*.
- Age-group competitions are open only to players of a similar age.

Ki-Young Jeon

Ki-Young Jeon *(left)* is South Korea's most successful *judoka* ever. He won the World Championships in the under-78 kg division in 1993, then moved up to the under-86 kg division to take world titles in 1995 and 1997. In between, he won the 1996 Olympic title as well.

Judo ranks

All *judokas*, from Olympic and World Champions to someone who has just joined a judo club for the first time, wear a colored belt. This shows everyone else their judo level, the number of techniques they have learned, and how effectively they are able to use them. A *judoka* earns promotion to a new rank by taking part in grading exams.

Getting a license

When new *judokas* join a judo club, they also join their national judo association. In many countries this guarantees a basic level of insurance, so that if a *judoka* is injured while fighting or practicing, he or she will be able to get compensation.

Joining the national association also gives *judoka* the right to take part in grading exams. This is where officials assess his or her progress and award new rankings—and perhaps a new belt color—if appropriate.

The younger members of this women's judo team should always be ready to listen to advice and guidance from their older, more experienced colleagues. This is one of the best ways for a young judoka *to learn the skills necessary to progress through the grades.*

Grades and exams

Juniors (usually fighters under the age of sixteen) have their own system of belt colors, which varies from country to country. A common one is described on page ten. Senior belt colors are the same all over the world.

Once a *judoka's* coach feels he or she is ready to move up a grade, the coach puts the person forward to take part in a grading exam. In this exam, two evenly matched *judokas* have a contest with each other under the gaze of judo officials. The aim is not so much to score points, as in a competition, but to demonstrate a variety of techniques. Of course, ideally this will result in a throw that would score *ippon* in a contest! After the contest is over, the officials make an assessment of how well the *judokas* have fought, and whether they have demonstrated particular techniques well enough that they should move up the grades.

Often a grading exam has a second part, where the *judoka* has to answer questions about judo. These questions may be about the theory and practice of the sport.

Young judoka *can be promoted by beating someone of a higher grade in a competition. They are then automatically raised to the same grade as the person they have beaten.*

Grading fact

One of the most important things in grading exams is to know judo's techniques well. Then it becomes possible to relax during the exam and pay attention to the referee's instructions.

Respect for other grades

Top-level *judoka* always show consideration for lower-graded fighters. Top fighters are much more likely to help them, by demonstrating a difficult technique, than to use their greater expertise to throw them around. This respect between the grades is an important part of judo, and it goes both ways. Lower-graded *judoka* must also show respect for the training and dedication that has gone into making another fighter a black belt, for example.

Being a champion *judoka*

World-class *judokas* get to travel the world, taking part in a sport they love. They train with the best coaches, in excellent facilities. Many receive financial and other help from their governments. Some *judoka* are sponsored by companies that want to be associated with successful athletes and appear on talk shows and as part of advertising campaigns. And, above all, judo champions are admired by other *judoka* around the world.

Many big-name judo stars get involved in high-profile charity work. Here David Douillet is pictured at the launch of an appeal to raise money for children in hospital in France.

Crab antics

If you put a load of crabs in a bucket, they try to escape. Up to a point, the crabs help each other. They pile up on one side of the bucket, climbing up on one another to get to the top. But as soon as one of the crabs gets close to escaping, the others stop helping and instead pull it back down.

Being a judo champion is a bit like being the crab nearest the top of the bucket. Everyone wants to beat you, and all the others are trying to pull you down. Whatever tournament you are at—whether it is the Olympics or a small local event—all eyes are on you, and every opponent is desperate to win a victory.

This means that a champion *judoka* has to train harder than ever, knowing that if he or she does not, somewhere out there a future opponent will be preparing to beat him or her. This pressure comes at exactly the time when training harder becomes more difficult, because of the *judoka's* other responsibilities.

Ryoko Tamura of Japan is surrounded by press photographers after winning gold at the 2000 Sydney Olympics.

Sponsorship

Commercial sponsors usually want something in return for their money. This might mean the *judoka* taking part in an advertising campaign, meeting clients of the sponsor, or making appearances for them at charity and other events. All these things take time from a champion's training schedule.

Life after competition

Once they have retired from competition, what does a former champion do? They will be free from the demands of training and competition, but many want to stay around the sport they love. As a result, some former champions stay in the world of judo. They find work as coaches, administrators, commentators, or journalists, putting their knowledge of the sport to use.

David Douillet, France

David Douillet of France *(pictured in the background)* is the most successful male *judoka* ever in international competition. He won Olympic heavyweight titles in 1996 and 2000, and the World Championships four times. In France he was also voted Sports Personality of the Year. Douillet is now retired from competition, and he coaches the French heavyweight team.

Recent champions

The tables below list the men's and women's champions in each weight division at the 2000 Sydney Olympics and the 2003 World Championships in Japan.

Men		
Weight category	**2000 Olympic champion**	**2003 World Champion**
Open	—	Keiji Suzuki (Japan)
> 100 kg	David Douillet (France)	Yasuyuki Muneta (Japan)
< 100 kg	Kosei Inoue (Japan)	Kosei Inoue (Japan)
< 90 kg	Mark Huizinga (Netherlands)	Hee-tae Hwang (South Korea)
< 81 kg	Makoto Takimoto (Japan)	Florian Wanner (Germany)
< 73 kg	Giuseppe Maddaloni (Italy)	Won Hee Lee (South Korea)
< 66 kg	Huseyin Ozkan (Turkey)	Arash Miresmaeili (Iran)
< 60 kg	Tadahiro Nomura (Japan)	Min-Ho Choi (South Korea)

Women		
Weight category	**2000 Olympic champion**	**2003 World Champion**
Open	—	Wen Tong (China)
> 78 kg	Hua Yuan (China)	Fuming Sun (China)
< 78 kg	Lin Tang (China)	Noriko Anno (Japan)
< 70 kg	Sibelis Veranes (Cuba)	Masae Ueno (Japan)
< 63 kg	Severine Vandenhende (France)	Daniela Krukower (Argentina)
< 57 kg	Isabel Fernandez (Spain)	Sun Hui Kye (North Korea)
< 52 kg	Legna Verdecia (Cuba)	Amarilis Savon (Cuba)
< 48 kg	Ryoko Tamura (Japan)	Ryoko Tamura (Japan)

Top ten most successful *judoka*, 1956–2001				
Name	**Country**	**World titles**	**Olympic titles**	**Total**
1. Ingrid Berghmans	Belgium	6	1	7
1. Ryoko Tamura	Japan	6	1	7
2. David Douillet	France	4	2	6
3. Yasuhiro Yamashita	Japan	4	1	5
4. Karen Briggs	Great Britain	4	0	4
4. Shozo Fuji	Japan	4	0	4
4. Fenglian Gao	China	4	0	4
4. Ki-Young Jeon	South Korea	3	1	4
4. Naoya Ogawa	Japan	4	0	4
4. Wilem Ruska	Netherlands	2	2	4

Judo terms

The judo terms below are all Japanese. When you see the letters "ai," you should pronounce them like the English word "eye."

dan black belt grades

dojo place where judo or another martial art is practiced and taught

gi pants, jacket, and belt for judo

harai goshi hip sweep

ippon a decisive score, awarded either for a throw in which the opponent lands with force on his or her back, a submission from an armlock, or a 25-second hold-down

judoka someone who practices judo

kansetsu waza armlocks

esa gatame a move known as the scarf hold, because the opponent's neck is wrapped up like a scarf

kohaku competition in which the winner stays on the mat until defeated

koka the lowest judo score possible, awarded for a throw where the opponent lands on the thigh or buttocks, or for a ten- to fifteen-second hold-down

koshi guruma hip wheel

kosoto gari small outer reap

kouchi gari small inner reap

umikata when a *judoka* grabs hold of his or her opponent

kuzushi techniques for breaking an opponent's balance

kyu judo grade

mon junior judo grade

morote gari two-handed reap

morote seoi nage two-handed shoulder throw

ogoshi large hip throw

osaekomi waza techniques to hold or pin down an opponent

osoto gari large outer reap

ouchi gari large inner reap

randori a session in which *judoka* are able to practice competition moves

renraku waza a combination technique

renzoku waza a linked technique

tai sabaki shifting body position to avoid being thrown

tatami judo mat

uchimata inner thigh reaping throw

ukemi techniques for lessening the impact of a fall

uki goshi a type of hip throw

waza-ari a half point, awarded either for a throw where the opponent lands partly on their side, or for a 21- to 25-second hold-down

yoko shiho gatame side-locking, four-corner hold

yuko a small score, awarded for a throw that lacks force or where the opponent lands on his or her side, or for a fifteen- to twenty-second hold-down

Glossary

application of power how *judokas* uses their own strength and the strength of their opponent when practicing different judo techniques

compensation payment made to make up for something difficult or bad that has happened

concentrated intense or especially heavy

demonstration sport sport that is being tried out at the Olympics or another competition, with the possibility of including it in the next games. The winners in demonstration sports are not awarded full Olympic medals.

Eastern bloc group of countries in central and eastern Europe, including Poland, the former Czechoslovakia, the former East Germany, Hungary, and Albania, that were governed by Communist rulers until the late 1980s

economy of movement describes the ability to perform an action in the most efficient way possible

feints pretend attacks, often designed to draw an opponent into making a move

flexibility ability to stretch muscles

momentum forward movement

muscle memory ability to reproduce a movement properly without thinking about it, because it has been practiced so many times already

nutrient substance that nourishes the growth or recovery of a living thing

reaction time amount of time it takes a person to react to physical or mental demands. A fighter who responds quickly to an attack, for example, has quick reaction times.

Soviet bloc countries in the former Soviet Union, including Russia, and those in the Eastern bloc

sponsored paid or given other rewards for taking part in an activity, usually in return for publicity. For example, a top *judoka* might be sponsored by a judo equipment manufacturer.

sweating down using high temperatures to lose moisture (and therefore weight) from the body through sweating. Some *judokas* do this to make sure they are light enough to compete in their chosen weight division.

weigh-in when *judokas* are weighed before competing in a judo match, to make sure they are not too heavy for their chosen weight division

Resources

Major international and U.S. organizations

USA Judo
One Olympic Plaza, Suite 202
Colorado Springs, Colo. 80909
719-866-4730

USJF-United States Judo Federation
P. O. Box 338
Ontario, Oreg. 97914
541-889-8753

IJF-International Judo Federation
33rd FL Doosan Tower, 18–12
Ulchi-Ro 6-Ka, Chung-Ku
Seoul, South Korea 100–300

IOC-International Olympic Committee
Château de Vidy
1007 Lausanne, Switzerland

*To find the organization's website, use a search engine and type in the organization's name as a keyword.

Further reading

Brousse, Michel. *A Century of Dedication, the History of Judo in America*. Ontario, Oreg.: United States Judo Federation, Inc., 2003.

Chesterman, Barnaby and Willingham, Bob. *Martial Arts: Judo*. Chicago: Raintree, 2003.

Collins, Paul. *Judo.* Broomall, Pa.: Chelsea House Publishers, 2001.

Janicot, Didier. *Judo Techniques and Tactics.* New York City: Sterling Publishing Co., 2000.

Morris, Neil. *Get Going! Martial Arts: Judo.* Chicago: Heinemann Library, 2001.

Sander, Hedda. *Judo: From White/Yellow Belt to Brown Belt*. Berkshire, England: Meyer & Meyer Sport, 2004.

Index